My
High
Times

An Hachette UK Company
www.hachette.co.uk

First published in Great Britain in 2013 by
Spruce, a division of Octopus Publishing Group Ltd
Endeavour House
189 Shaftesbury Avenue
London
WC2H 8JY
www.octopusbooks.co.uk
www.octopusbooks.usa.com

Distributed in the US by
Hachette Book Group USA
237 Park Avenue
New York NY 10017 USA

Distributed in Canada by
Canadian Manda Group
165 Dufferin Street
Toronto, Ontario, Canada M6K 3H6

ISBN 978-1-84601-426-0

A CIP catalogue record for this book is available from the British Library

Printed and bound in China

10 9 8 7 6 5 4 3 2 1

My High Times

A JOURNAL

FOR ALL YOUR GREATEST STONED IDEAS, STUPID
QUOTES, AND PLANS FOR WORLD DOMINATION

spruce

CONTENTS

INTRODUCTION

Marijuana is a mind-altering drug that has been used by holy men, artists, musicians, and even politicians (but we won't hold that against poor Mary Jane), for thousands of years. It chills you out, lets down your inhibitions, and sharpens your perception. You can find joy in pretty much anything—your friend's weird hairstyle that's longer on one side than the other, trying to paint your toenails (that goes for boys and girls, this is the 21st century, thankyouverymuch), watching three hours of YouTube videos of pandas sneezing, or trying to make your pet cat wear a hat (more on that later).

Anyone who's been stoned knows that after a spliff you feel just that little bit better about the world, and it can inspire you to acts of both unbelievable stupidity and incredible genius. When you're high, the world is your tiny, stoned little oyster.

This book is designed to help you make the most of that feeling by giving you somewhere to channel those creative energies.

How to use this book

The "My High Times" pages are journal-style entries where you can record the best bits of a particular stoner session, with just a little something extra for your blitzed brain to chew on.

"High Design" is a place to draw, sketch, and deface as you see fit, everything from T-shirts to bongs to world-changing inventions. And if you've ever seen a blockbuster movie, festival, or comic book hero and thought "I could totally do that," well, on the "I Could Totally Do That" pages, now's your chance, big shot.

There are games and puzzles for pot-lovers, too, as well as some recipes using very special ingredients, and ideas for when you want to host a hash party. Use these pages to record your personal highs— your best ideas; your best smokes; your best friends (and the stupid things they say when they're toasted)—so that they're all there in black and white for when you want to relive the memories (or for blackmailing purposes).

Of course, with all good things (except ponies), weed is best served in reasonably small packages, and nobody knows this better than Mr Whitey. Mr Whitey is the very cat that I tried to make look good in the hat (I'll let you be the judge), and he also ate an entire quarter block of resin when I wasn't looking. He's never been the same since.

I guess there's a lesson for us all there. Enjoy in moderation, and don't force it on dumb animals.

COOKING WITH CANNABIS

Throughout this book you'll find a number of heavenly hash recipes that are guaranteed to spice up your time in the kitchen. "But wait!" I hear you cry. "I've only got weed! That guy sold me skunk! I'm stuck with Pepe le Pew!"

Worry not, my friends! If you don't have any hash to hand (that's the sticky resin stuff, usually sold in a ball), then you can adapt the recipe in a few easy steps to work equally well with the dry herbal stuff, thanks to the wonder of Cannabutter!

Cannabutter is simple (if a bit time consuming) to make, but you can make a batch and store it in the freezer. (Freezing it means it doesn't lose its edge.) All you need to do with the recipes is ignore the "hash" bit, replace the quantity of normal butter with Cannabutter, and you're laughing! Probably hysterically!

Cannabutter

- 1 oz cannabis (as good as your dealer will give you)
- 2 cups water
- 2 cups unsalted butter

1. Grind the cannabis to a fine powder using a strong grinder.

2. Pour 2 cups of water into a heavy saucepan and bring to a steady boil over medium-high heat. Once boiling, add the butter and melt it in the water. Reduce the heat to very low and then beat in the cannabis powder until thoroughly combined. Cover and let simmer very, very gently for around 22 hours. Check on the butter mixture every couple of hours

to ensure that the simmer is not too strong and the butter has not reduced too much. If you find the solution reducing faster than expected, add a couple of tablespoons of water.

3. Once the butter has simmered for long enough, turn off the heat and let stand for 2–4 minutes. Meanwhile, place a large square of cheesecloth over a bowl. (Leave enough cloth on either side so that it doesn't fall in!) Pour the butter mixture through the cheesecloth, straining off all the cannabis. Once the butter has been strained, gather the edges of the cheesecloth and carefully squeeze the cannabis residue to extract as much butter as possible. Discard the cheesecloth. (All that cannabis goodness is in the butter now!)

4. Place the bowl of butter mixture in your refrigerator and let cool for a few hours or overnight, until the fats have separated from the water. Using heavy-duty plastic wrap, remove the top slab of now solid Cannabutter from the bowl, and pat dry with paper towel to remove any excess water.

5. Cut the butter into smaller portions, about 1 stick per portion, and compress with plastic wrap. Store any extra packets in the freezer.

Congratulations! You now have the power to turn any old boring recipe into a gourmet ganja dish! Just don't spring it on any unsuspecting old timers—it makes for a surprisingly powerful (if slow burning) high.

TOKES OF GENIUS

It's the same old story.

You've kicked back with a spliff or a sneaky hash brownie, you've let your body relax and your mind wander and suddenly, WHAM! You've had an epiphany. This is a great idea. The greatest of great ideas. This is going to change the world. All you need to do now is find a pen … but that would mean getting out of this comfy, comfy chair.

Never mind. It's fine … you can't have an idea this phenomenal, this monumentally earth shattering, this astronomically, fundamentally brilliant, and not remember what it was.

Five minutes pass. You're scrabbling about in the fridge for something to go on top of a grilled cheese sandwich (ANSWER: MORE CHEESE) and wondering whether that album you put on has finished already, or whether you ever started it in the first place. The idea has gone forever, and the world's been deprived of a little bit of genius. Oh well, at least you've got your cheese sandwich, I guess.

NO MORE.

(I mean, you can still have your grilled cheese, but no more forgetting.)

Over to you

Before we get started with the nitty gritty of nuts drawings, wacky puzzles, and generally great, fun stuff to do while you're half-baked, remember these pages, nicely and conveniently here at the front of the journal. Because it's right here that you should write down all those wham, bam, thank you ma'am moments of blissful inspiration, without having to scrimmage around to see whether there's a special page for crazy inventions (see page 28), your ultimate superhero costume (see page 93), or that incredible idea you had for a strain of cannabis (see page 40). Once they're safe in here, you can look them up when the purple haze has cleared and bask in the knowledge that you, my friend, are almost certainly a genius.*

I MUST remember who said that.
The $64,000 question.

"Buy the ticket, take the ride."
Hunter S. Thompson

"Much virtue in herbs, little in men."
Benjamin Franklin

My lightbulb moment. Ping!

STONED ALONE

There is something to be said for getting stoned alone. Suddenly ten minutes feels like two hours, you can have some pretty crazy ideas (some of which might be pretty good—in which case write it down, quick!), and you can have some quality "ME ME ME" time, which all the self-help books recommend. Whether you use cannabis to just kick back and relax after a tough day or to help you get creative, it can be even more satisfying having a session where you don't have to share with anybody else. With snacks to take the edge off, smoking skills for practice, and pages and pages of idea-inspiring things to do, this is the bit of the book for you, and only you.

Feel special, man.

MY HIGH TIMES

What's the occasion?

How'd you get high?

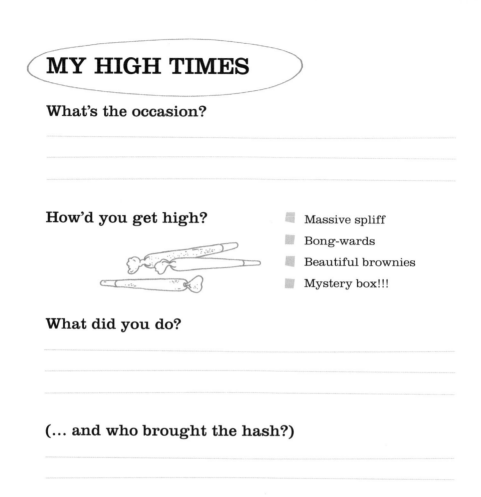

- Massive spliff
- Bong-wards
- Beautiful brownies
- Mystery box!!!

What did you do?

(... and who brought the hash?)

Best highs

Any lows?

List some of your favorite things to do when you're flying solo

* take a bath
* stare at stuff
* draw
* bust mad rhymes
* EAT

HOW HIGH AM I?

When you're sparking up with friends, there will always be somebody there to tell you when you've hit your limit. There are some pretty obvious signs that you're getting high that you can spot yourself (even when your observational skills are somewhat "incapacitated") and these are well documented by stoners the world over:

- A nice, warm buzz.
- A lot of things start having the potential to be **hilarious**.
- A case of the munchies.

But everyone's got their own personal route down the rabbit hole, and sometimes it's nice to figure out just how far you've gone. Below are some pretty good indications.

You've invented a religion.

You've set your shoe on fire.

You've already eaten three bags of chips.

You thought the sirens in a song were an actual police cruiser.

The radio is talking to you—and you're talking back.

You've just spent 15 minutes on the phone to the pizza delivery place.

Brushing your teeth feels AMAZING.

This book feels pretty damn heavy.

You're staring at the TV, and it's not even on.

You've needed the bathroom for like two hours now.

Your sentences are one word long.

Fill in your own half-cut mishaps to create your personal sliding scale of stonedness.

RECIPE

Breakfast of champions

What better way to start the day than as you mean to go on—by getting absolutely blitzed before you've even had your morning coffee? These chronic-spiced blueberry pancakes make the perfect pothead breakfast, and will definitely keep you going until lunch.

- $\frac{1}{16}$ oz blond hash
- 1 cup self-rising flour
- Finely grated zest of $\frac{1}{2}$ lemon
- 1 teaspoon baking powder
- 1 tablespoon superfine sugar
- 1 egg
- 1 tablespoon freshly squeezed lemon juice
- $\frac{2}{3}$ cup low-fat milk
- Generous $\frac{3}{4}$ cup blueberries
- Oil, for pan-frying
- Maple syrup
- Ice cream, to serve

Makes 10

1. Put the hash, flour, lemon zest, baking powder, and sugar into a mixing bowl. Add the egg and lemon juice, then gradually beat in the milk until you have a smooth, thick batter. Stir in the blueberries, reserving a few for decoration.

2. Heat a griddle or large skillet, then rub it with a piece of paper towel drizzled with a little oil. Drop spoonfuls of the mixture, well spaced apart, on the griddle or skillet and cook for 2–3 minutes until bubbles form on the surface and the underside is golden brown.

3. Turn the pancakes over and cook the reverse side. Wrap in a dish cloth and keep warm while you cook the remainder of the mixture in the same way. Stack 3 or 4 pancakes on each plate and drizzle with maple syrup. Decorate with the reserved blueberries and serve with ice cream.

My testing and tasting notes

_____

_____

_____

_____

_____

_____

_____

WHO ATE ALL THE PANCAKES?

My top 10 breakfasts

1 _____
2 _____
3 _____
4 _____
5 _____
6 _____
7 _____
8 _____
9 _____
10 _____

HOW TO ROLL A TULIP

A favorite of the coffee shops in Amsterdam, this miracle of nature also packs a powerful punch. As the bulb gets wider, your hits get stronger, so be careful to mix your weed well before you begin. Also, don't scrimp on the stem—you need the length to allow all that sweet smoke to cool before it gets to your mouth.

Flower power

1. Make an über-roach roughly the length and width of a pen. You can use thin card for this, but it's best to make sure it doesn't have any weird colors or finishes on it. Seal the tube with two large papers.

2. Take two more large papers and overlap them slightly to form a square.

3. Fold the upper, right-hand corner of the square toward the lower, left-hand corner, just before the gummed strip.

4. Lick the gummed strip and fold over. Squeeze the edges gently to make a cone, and fill with a thoroughly blended mixture of tobacco and weed up to about two-thirds high (don't get too greedy, now!).

5. Gather together the excess paper at the top of the cone, and insert the roach into the top. Remember: gently, gently, catchy monkey.

6. Scrunch the paper tightly around the top of the roach, and tie off with thread or an elastic band. It's important to keep this as tight as possible.

Make like you're in Amsterdam, light up, and watch that tulip bloom!

I COULD TOTALLY DO THAT

Conceptual art

Yes, the weed has inspired and empowered you to channel your creative side. You can see the beauty in everything—the subtle form of that chair leg, the intricate texture of your couch cushions, the sugar glistening on the top of that pop tart. So what if the last thing you drew was a cat that looked like a monster truck when you were seven years old? Thanks to the fast-moving modern art world, all you need now to become a major player is an **idea**. So watch out Warhol, roll over Rothko, things are about to get arty.

What's your message?

* futility of youth
* antiwar
* post-post-post-modernism
* isolation
* kitties

Pick a publicity stunt for opening night

What's your medium?

_____

_____

_____

_____

_____

_____

* lion dung
* modeling-clay
* vegetables
* watercolor
* biro from the
  back of the couch

Sketch your masterpiece here

HIGH DESIGN

Inventions

- The printing press.
- Electricity.
- Toilets.
- The post-it note.

These are some of the greatest inventions of humankind. What better way to add to the list of revolutionary, life-altering inventions than by using a mind-altering drug? Whether it's a cure for the common cold or a doohickey for making sure the toilet paper is always the right way round, think about what the world's missing ... and invent it!

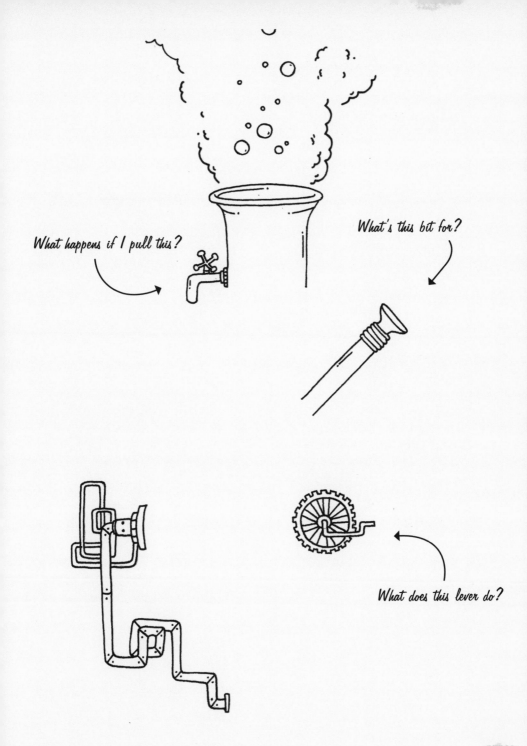

What happens if I pull this?

What's this bit for?

What does this lever do?

MY HIGH TIMES

What's the occasion?

_____

_____

How'd you get high?

- Massive spliff
- Bong-wards
- Beautiful brownies
- Mystery box!!!

What did you do?

_____

_____

_____

(... and who brought the hash?)

_____

_____

Best highs

_____

_____

_____

_____

_____

_____

Any lows?

Soundtrack

All music sounds great when you're high (except Country and Western—there's nothing anybody can do about that), but what are your favorite songs to listen to?

HOW TO BLOW A SMOKE RING

Smoke rings are possibly the greatest party trick on this earth. If anybody tells you they don't care about being able to blow smoke rings (smoker or not), they are lying through their non-smoke-ring-blowing teeth. It's an art form that makes you instantly cooler if you get it right—girls look hot doing it, guys look suave—but get it wrong and you just look like a drowning guppy with its mouth on fire. So it's a trick that requires some solo practice first.

Price of perfection

The thing about smoke rings is that they require you **not** to inhale, so in some ways, they're a pothead's worst enemy! But sometimes a stoner's got to suffer for his art.

This works best with dense smoke, so don't mix with light tobacco. Make up a decent-sized fatty and, crucially, make sure it's as densely packed as possible. Alternatively, use a cigarette and tap it to make sure the tobacco packs as close as possible to the filter end.

1. Take a few drags to get the smoke going and the joint as hot as possible. Take a big drag and DON'T INHALE. Hold the smoke in the back of your mouth/top of your throat. This bit takes practice, and might make even a veteran stoner cough a bit. No shame.

2. Position your tongue toward the bottom of your mouth, slightly pointed. Make an "Ooo" (as in "Oooh baby," not "Oh no!") shape with your lips, keeping the shape as wide as possible.

3. Release a small puff of smoke from the back of your mouth, exhaling slightly. Some people find dropping the jaw down and forward at the crucial moment also helps—as though you were saying "Uh."

4. Watch and wait as adoring acolytes flock to your stoner circle.

Remember, practice makes perfect.

WARNING:
Blowing smoke rings can make you look seriously cool.

RECIPE

Peanut butter cookies

A glass of milk and one of these freshly baked cookies will definitely send you straight to sleep. A word to the wise—if this is the only food in the house, then halve the dough before adding the hash to one half, so that you've got some virgin cookies available too (make it clear which is which once you've baked them!). Trying to stave off the munchies with these bad boys is like a shipwrecked man drinking seawater, and you'll probably be in bed for a month.

- 9 tablespoons (1^{1}/$_{8}$ sticks) unsalted butter, softened
- ^{3}/$_{4}$ cup light brown sugar
- Scant ^{1}/$_{2}$ cup chunky peanut butter
- ^{1}/$_{7}$ oz black hash
- 1 egg, lightly beaten
- 1^{1}/$_{4}$ cups all-purpose flour
- ^{1}/$_{2}$ teaspoon baking powder
- Generous ^{3}/$_{4}$ cup unsalted peanuts

Makes **28**

1. Preheat the oven to 375°F. Lightly grease three large cookie sheets.

2. Put the butter and sugar in a mixing bowl and beat together until pale and creamy. Add the peanut butter, hash, egg, flour, and baking powder and mix together until combined. Stir in the peanuts.

3. Take large teaspoonfuls of the dough and position on the cookie sheets, leaving a good 2-inch gap between them to allow for spreading. Flatten slightly.

4. Bake in the preheated oven for 12 minutes or until the cookies are golden around the edges. Let cool slightly on the cookie sheets for a few minutes and then transfer to a cooling rack to cool completely.

Anyone for high tea?

To make Masala Chai to serve with your cookies, put
6 teaspoons Darjeeling tea leaves, 1 cup milk, ¼ teaspoon
each of ground ginger and crushed cardamom seeds,
$\frac{1}{8}$ teaspoon ground cloves, 1 cinnamon stick, 1 tablespoon
sugar, 4 cups water and $\frac{1}{14}$ oz hash into a large saucepan
over a medium heat. Bring to a rolling boil, then reduce the
heat to low and simmer for 5–6 minutes. Strain into four large
mugs or glasses and serve hot.

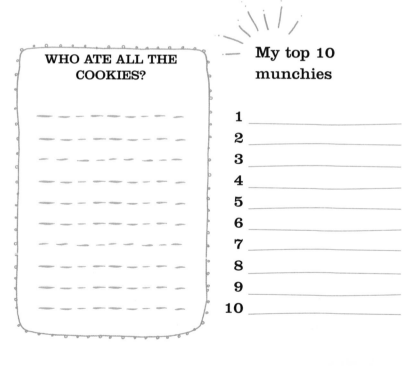

WHO ATE ALL THE COOKIES?

My top 10 munchies

1 _____
2 _____
3 _____
4 _____
5 _____
6 _____
7 _____
8 _____
9 _____
10 _____

HIGH-KU

Using just five syllables, then seven, then five, the haiku is one of the most ancient and profound forms of Japanese poetry. By describing two arresting images, the poem captures a poignant and resonant moment or idea. And moments don't get much more resonant than when you're high! When you get fixated on something totally bizarre and can't get it out of your head—that, my friend, is the start of something beautiful.

Reefer rhymes

Put pen to paper, let your creative juices flow, and share your literary gift with the world.

A cat in a hat
In a room full of stoners.
He suddenly barfs.

HIGH DESIGN

Scary monsters

Smoked responsibly, cannabis is nothing to get scared about. But sometimes, if you get a bad strain of hash, you eat one too many bad-ass brownies, or you otherwise overdo it, it can give you a serious case of the heebie-jeebies. Ward off your willies by confronting your fears and drawing the ugliest, most hideous, terrifying monster you can think of in the space opposite: creepy claws, nasty slimy scales, math professor eyes—the works.

Express your innermost fears here.

39

NAME ... THAT ... WEED!

Whether it's homegrown or hailing from sunny Amsterdam, made in Morocco or farmed in Nepal, resin or hash, skunk or bud, there are all sorts of types and strains of cannabis, and even more names for them. Some are slang that's as old as the hills: weed, marijuana, spliffs, tokes. Others are old familiar characters like Mary Jane and Alice B. But plenty more names for cannabis change with the times, and you don't want to get caught out! Stay ahead of the street slang by inventing your own.

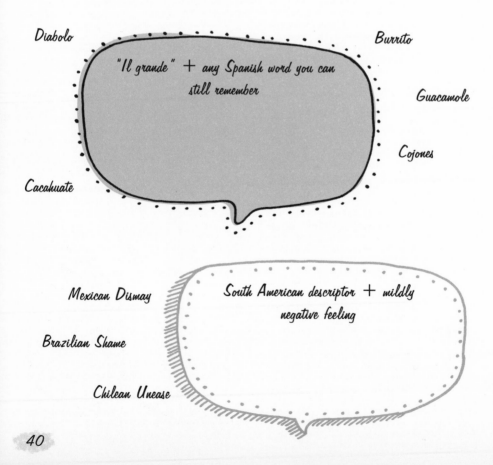

Diabolo

Burrito

"Il grande" + any Spanish word you can still remember

Guacamole

Cojones

Cacahuate

Mexican Dismay

South American descriptor + mildly negative feeling

Brazilian Shame

Chilean Unease

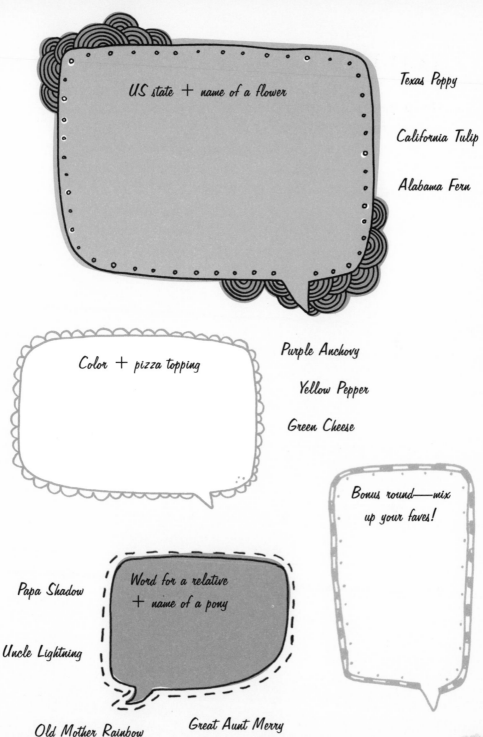

US state + name of a flower

Texas Poppy

California Tulip

Alabama Fern

Color + pizza topping

Purple Anchovy

Yellow Pepper

Green Cheese

Bonus round—mix up your faves!

Papa Shadow

Uncle Lightning

Word for a relative + name of a pony

Old Mother Rainbow

Great Aunt Merry

41

I COULD TOTALLY DO THAT

Soap opera

Not just for crazy grandmas and angry rednecks! If you've ever got so bombed out of your skull that the next day all you can do is lie on the couch watching TV, chances are you've encountered your fair share of soap operas. Glamorous women, suave older men, precocious teens, blackmail, affairs, and betrayal—and all safe in the knowledge that you don't need to have a clue what's going on as it'll all change by the end of the episode anyway. Smoke a hair of the dog and concoct your own glitzy daytime soap for stoners like you to while away the day with.

Title

Get some characters

Troy Jackhammer

Algernon Weasel

Misty Morning

Brooke Rogers

Penny Golightly

Bobby Valentino

Ol' Rusty

Tell us a bit about them

Mama Whitey loves her stories.

Where's it set?

Who's the baddie?

Who's having an affair?

Who's the secret love child?

Series cliffhanger

* car crash
* evil twin
* amnesia
* rock slide
* gunshot
* alien abduction

MY HIGH TIMES

What's the occasion?

How'd you get high?

- Massive spliff
- Bong-wards
- Beautiful brownies
- Mystery box!!!

What did you do?

(... and who brought the hash?)

Best highs

Any lows?

**If you could go anywhere in the world,
right now, where would it be?**

_____

_____

_____

_____

_____

Who would you take with you?

_____

_____

_____

Favorite way to get there

_____ * skateboard

_____ * jet pack

_____ * pedalo

_____ * surfboard

What would you do?

_____

_____

_____

_____

HIGH DESIGN

T-shirt

Don't pretend you don't want to. Every douchebag with a graphic design major is doing it and charging $20 a pop, so why shouldn't you? Trawl no more through aisles of identikit shirts to find the slogan that sums up your post-ironic take on life. That Che shirt has probably had its day. Design your own.

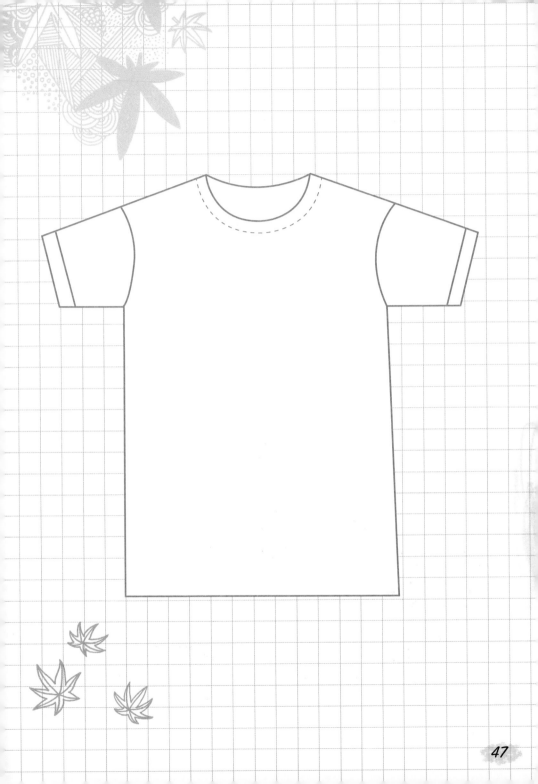

SPOT THE DIFFERENCE

Who doesn't love a game of spot the difference? A childhood game to sharpen your wits and hone your powers of perception. Plus, when you're half-baked, it makes things a whole lot more interesting. You could be here for hours! See if you can discover the differences between these two heartwarming portraits of Mr Whitey during a post-apocalyptic zombie outbreak. If you get stuck, check page 112 for the answers.

If Zombie Whitey is freaking you out, turn to page 70 and make an escape plan.

OUT & ABOUT

Whether you're headed to catch a movie, on your way home from work, or just chilling out in the park, this section is for the pothead going places. Obviously getting stoned in public is a high-risk activity, so there are plenty of cannabis recipes to keep your stash a secret, plus the chance to design your own super sneaky disguises. It's also got places to keep track of all your people watching and plans for world domination as you go about your daily business.

MY HIGH TIMES

What's the occasion?

How'd you get high?

- Massive spliff
- Bong-wards
- Beautiful brownies
- Mystery box!!!

What did you do?

(… and who brought the hash?)

Best highs

Any lows?

Best places to hang out when you're high

Best munchies in town

Places to avoid

* outside the police station
* school gates
* middle of the highway

I COULD TOTALLY DO THAT

Rule the world

There is nothing like going out into the world with a bit of THC in your system to change your take on how things are done. Things'd be very different if you were in charge though, I bet. Oh yes, veeeery different .... Indulge your inner megalomaniac and think about how you'd run the show. But would you use your powers for good or evil?

Your title

(every self-respecting world leader has to have one):

Your Worthiness

Majordomo

Most Righteous

Grand High Vizier

(Inter)National anthem

On a scale of 1 to evil, I would be

My First Lady/Man would be

Official portrait

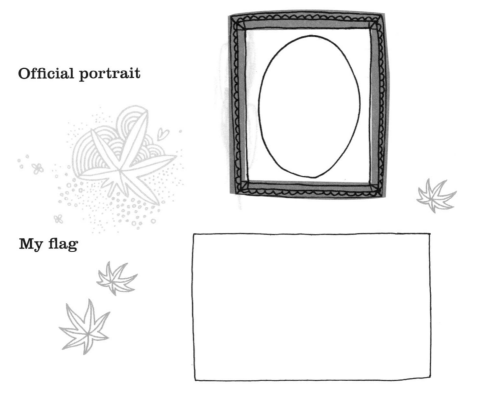

My flag

It would be compulsory to

And against the law to

Defining moment in history

HIGH DESIGN

Planet

Feeling out of this world? If you're flying higher than
a kite right now, then put pen to intergalactic paper
and sketch what planet you're on. Trace your travels
through outer space (and fill in any adventures on the way).
It doesn't **even** have to bear any relation to anything you learned
(or didn't learn) about the solar system in class.

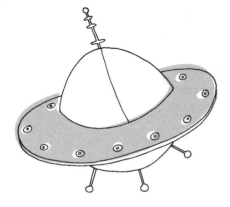

Draw your own spaceship
and don't forget the vitals
(jacuzzi/movie theater/bean
bag chairs ...)

How about alien
life forms?

RECIPE

Oaty hash bars

One of the benefits of eating, as opposed to smoking, your hash is that you avoid the telltale smell that tends to attract the authorities. Plus it sidesteps that pesky lung cancer issue. So, these hash-flavored oat bars are the perfect scooby snack for when you're on the road. As innocent-and-wholesome-looking as Laura Ingalls Wilder, no one will ever suspect they'll get you high as a kite, with not a bong or a baggie in sight. Oaty hash bars are a great addition to a bagged lunch that packs a punch (just don't expect to get much work done).

- $1/7$ oz black hash
- 7 tablespoons margarine
- $1/2$ cup white vegetable fat
- Generous $1/2$ cup turbinado sugar
- 4 tablespoons light corn syrup
- $3^1/2$ cups rolled oats

Makes 16

1. Preheat the oven to 325°F. Grease a 13 x 9 x 2-inch baking pan and line the base with parchment paper.

2. Put the hash, margarine, vegetable fat, sugar, and corn syrup in a medium saucepan. Stir over a low heat until the margarine and fat are melted and the sugar has dissolved. Remove from the heat and stir in the rolled oats until evenly coated.

3. Transfer the mixture to the prepared baking pan and spread it out, gently pressing it down so the surface is even.

4. Bake in the preheated oven for 35 minutes or until the mixture is deep golden all over. Remove from the oven and immediately score into 16 slices. Let cool in the pan and then cut into slices.

My top 10 scooby snacks

1 _____
2 _____
3 _____
4 _____
5 _____
6 _____
7 _____
8 _____
9 _____
10 _____

WHO ATE ALL THE HASH BARS?

HOW TO ROLL A SPLIFFARETTE

If you love the herb but miss the suavity, sophistication, and downright coolness of having an old-fashioned cigarette in your hands, then this is a cigarette with a sneaky twist. With a sleight of hand worthy of 007 himself, this little trick joint looks exactly like a regular smoke to the casual observer, and is so convincing you could happily spark up in public ... so long as they don't figure out what that smell is.

The perfect disguise

1. Take two large papers and overlap them slightly to form a square.

2. Remove the filter from your cigarette by squeezing at the base and rotating slightly with your finger and thumb. It's fiddly work, but the filter should eventually come out.

3. When it does, replace the filter with a trusty roach of the same size.

4. Cut the cigarette with a sharp knife or scissors, about ½ inch from the roach end. Lay this on your rolling square.

5. Mix your weed with the tobacco from the rest of the cigarette, and roll the joint with your roach sticking out of the end.

6. If it's a little rough around the edges, use a gummed strip from another rolling paper to secure the roach. Et voilà! Doesn't it look just like a cigarette? Just remember, it don't smell like one.

PEOPLE WATCHING

If you're out and about after a spliff (or maybe some delicious pancakes, see Breakfast of Champions, page 22), then indulging in a bit of people watching can take on a whole new dimension. Passers-by you wouldn't normally give a second glance suddenly become fascinating characters and whatever they're carrying, or whoever they're with, will have a new-found significance.

Use these pages to jot down the best experiences you've had people watching while high. I mean, it probably wouldn't win you the Pulitzer, but whatever, it's a start.

* Who's got a great hat?
* Who could be a spy?
* Who's a secret serial killer?

Wear shades if you don't want to end up eyeballing someone.

* What's up with her?
* What's their story?
* What's his favorite pizza topping?

MY HIGH TIMES

What's the occasion?

How'd you get high?

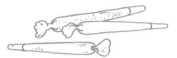

- Massive spliff
- Bong-wards
- Beautiful brownies
- Mystery box!!!

What did you do?

(... and who brought the hash?)

Best highs

Any lows?

Anybody make a total fool of themselves?

Name and shame

Ideal pothead picnic

Disguises

It's a sad fact of the stoner's life that you're perpetually living on the wrong side of the law (or in the Netherlands). You're a soldier of fortune, surviving by your wits, dodging the feds, and sticking it to the Man. But for those times you really need to keep things on the down-low and the Q.T., you're gonna need a cunning disguise.

Sketch some stealthy shades…

… and your incognito hat.

Now for the full-body disguise. If you're stuck for
something that isn't your normal jeans and T-shirt,
try an all-out costume. No one will suspect a thing.
You could draw some inspiration from your superhero
alter ego (see page 92).

I COULD TOTALLY DO THAT

Movie mogul

It's a Saturday night at the movies and you've popped more than the popcorn. Perhaps this laugh-a-minute bromance/kooky comedy with the mismatched cop duo/ditzy bangs/CGI bunny is going to be bearable after all. But then, a flash of inspiration hits: I COULD TOTALLY DO THIS. You could. You could totally do this.

What will it be?

- Romcom
- Action movie
- Cartoon
- Buddy
- Fantasy
- Genre-busting

Get some characters

Hank Muscleman

Bubbles

Lucy Lovebegone

Best Pal Dave

Scaly Pete

Joe Shrapnel

Lady Garden

My leading lady and Hollywood heartthrob

Scenarios

Loses their job as a

_____

_____

* *hot dog vendor*
* *stock trader*

Finds an enchanted

_____

_____

* *mask*
* *sword*

Has to save the world from

_____

_____

* *killer bee*
* *evil astronaut*

Draw your movie poster here

Cast list

_____

_____

_____

_____

_____

_____

_____

_____

_____

ZOMBIE ESCAPE PLAN

Sure, pot makes you paranoid, but sometimes it pays to be prepared. Yeah, everybody else might make fun of you, but the day that there's no more room in hell and the dead start walking the earth, you, my friend, will be the one laughing, as you hot foot it with a select group of survivors away from the zombie menace. Figure out now who and what you're taking and where you'll go, and you'll be halfway to an underground bunker before you can say, "Aim for the head!"

Who're you taking with you?
(Yes, survival skills are important, but so is not spending eternity with someone who sets your teeth on edge. Snores attract zombies!)

What will you pack?
(apart from your stash, obviously)

Where will you go?
(the mall is a classic, but it hardly ever ends well)

Weapon of choice

- Camper van
- Baseball bat
- AK-47
- Crossbow
- Hole punch
- Chainsaw
- DIY contraption

Draw your contraption

Romantic interest

(**somebody's** got to repopulate the world)

Braaaaaaaaaa aaaaaaaaaaaaaaaains

Is there room for survivors?

(you don't want to be a dick, but there's only so much space in a car)

Who to avoid

(authority-crazed sheriffs, charismatic cult leaders, etc.)

MY HIGH TIMES

What's the occasion?

How'd you get high?

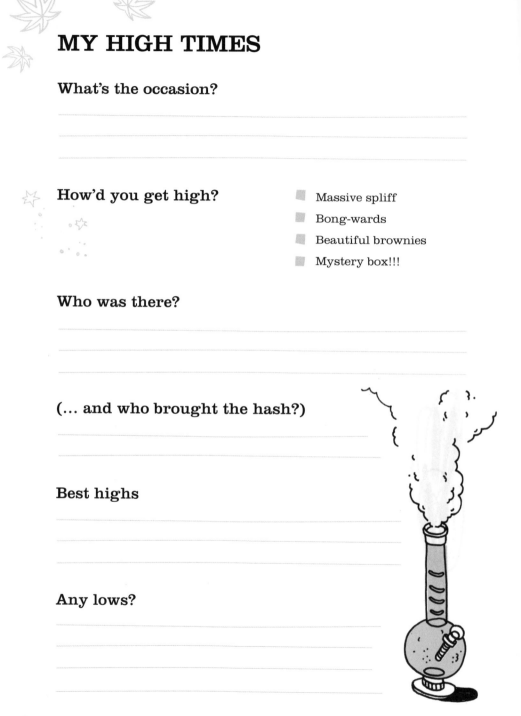

- Massive spliff
- Bong-wards
- Beautiful brownies
- Mystery box!!!

Who was there?

(... and who brought the hash?)

Best highs

Any lows?

List your favorite stoner movies

_____

_____

_____

_____

_____

_____

_____

_____

_____

... and movies to watch stoned

(or maybe they're the same thing)

_____

_____

_____

_____

_____

_____

_____

_____

_____

_____

_____

RECIPE

Mary Jane's cherry pie

There's nothing quite like a warm cup of Joe (thanks Joe!) and a slice of all-American cherry pie. And there's definitely nothing quite like *this* cherry pie. Pack it for a pothead picnic in the park, and watch the clouds go by. You'll be sky high in no time.

- 13¼ oz sweet shortcrust pastry
- 1⅔ cups fresh or frozen cherries (pitted if fresh, thawed if frozen)
- 2 tablespoons granulated sugar
- ¹⁄₁₆ oz black hash
- Milk, to glaze
- ½ cup slivered almonds, to decorate
- Heavy cream, to serve

Serves 6

1. Roll out about two-thirds of the pastry on a lightly floured work surface and use to line a 9-inch tart pan. Chill in the refrigerator for 30 minutes.

2. Preheat the oven to 375°F. Spread the cherries evenly over the pastry case, and sprinkle with the sugar and hash.

3. Roll out the remaining pastry and cut it into thin strips. Brush the rim of the tart with

Mmm ... just like Mama Whitey used to make.

74

water and arrange the pastry strips in a lattice pattern over the top of the cherries. Brush the pastry with a little milk and sprinkle the pie with the slivered almonds.

4. Bake in the preheated oven for 30–35 minutes or until the pastry is golden and the cherries are tender. Serve warm or cold with heavy cream.

WHO ATE ALL THE CHERRY PIE?

My top 10 pie fillings

1 _____
2 _____
3 _____
4 _____
5 _____
6 _____
7 _____
8 _____
9 _____
10 _____

DREAM JOB

"Get a job!" is something that every self-respecting stoner will at some point have to hear, whether it's their mother calling from the top of the stairs (and to be fair, maybe 35 is a bit old to be living in the basement) or a passer-by who takes issue with you and your friends hanging out outside the 7-Eleven on a Tuesday afternoon. Well, anyone who says this book is irresponsible should think again, as you're about to get a hit of some Grade A careers advisory guidance right here.

Use these pages (and a bit of "lateral" thinking) to figure out your dream job—one that requires minimum work, maximum satisfaction, and a boss who won't mind if you take a quick toke now and again.

* Gangster rapper
* Carnival ride operator
* Freak show freak
* Food taster for popular royalty
* Board game inventor
* Video game tester
* Guinea-pig whisperer

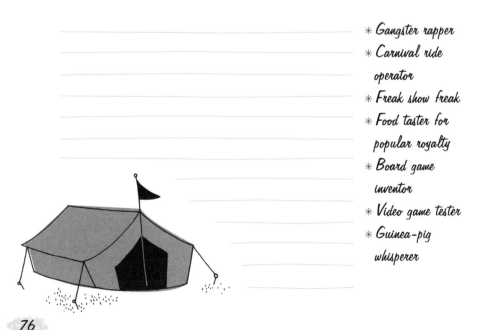

Employee of the Month

AMAZING MAZES!

Try this stoner twist on a kids' classic. Find your way to the delicious munchies before you eat something you regret! But remember, getting to the kitchen is harder than it looks when you're half-baked already...

PARTY TIME!

Of course, like a fine wine, sometimes the best way to appreciate a quality hash (or even a substandard, dried up bit of weed you found in the back of your sock drawer) is with friends. This section is for the greatest schemes, the stupidest stunts, and the best moments you've had with your **compadres** smoking by your side. Packed with your personal pot party planner (try saying that after a blunt), games, and finger food with a little extra "spice," this is everything you'll need for an unforgettable (well, maybe not) night on an herbal high.

PARTY PLANNER

So, you're setting up a pot party? Excellent! There's really not much more that you need than some good quality ganja and a few friends, but sometimes if it's a special occasion you might want to get organized beforehand. That way, on the night you don't have to worry about a thing (especially useful if you're in a trance in the corner).

What's the occasion?

_____

_____

Guest list

_____

_____

_____

_____

_____

* Who barfed last time?
* Who never brings his own stash?

Playlist

_____

_____

_____

_____

_____

_____

_____

_____

Ground rules

_____

_____

_____

_____

_____

_____

_____

* Smoke what
  you bring
* Sharing's caring!
* No mixing bongs
  and booze
* Sleep where
  you fall

Games/diversions/
forfeits/activities

Make a plan now because
you'll never remember
the rules later.

_____

_____

_____

_____

_____

_____

_____

MENU CARD

- – – – – – – – –
- – – – – – – – –
- – – – – – – – –
- – – – – – – – –
- – – – – – – – –
- – – – – – – – –
- – – – – – – – –
- – – – – – – – –
- – – – – – – – –
- – – – – – – – –
- – – – – – – – –
- – – – – – – – –

RECIPE

Hash brownies

The delicious foundations on which any self-respecting pot party is built, these hash brownies are the Adam and Eve, the Big Bang, the bread and butter (but a lot tastier) of culinary cannabis. Also known as space cakes or Alice B. Toklas (she was Gertrude Stein's squeeze, a 1920s literary icon, and famous for her excellent chronic cookery skills), these moreish morsels are a guaranteed hit at any gathering.

- 7 oz bittersweet chocolate, broken into chunks
- 14 tablespoons ($1^3/4$ sticks) unsalted butter
- 3 eggs
- 1 teaspoon vanilla extract
- 1 tablespoon strong espresso (or 1 tablespoon coffee granules dissolved in 1 tablespoon hot water)
- 1 cup superfine sugar
- $3/4$ cup all-purpose flour
- $1/4$ teaspoon salt
- $1/7$ oz black hash
- $2/3$ cup walnuts, roughly chopped
- $2/3$ cup pecan nuts, roughly chopped

Makes 12–16

1. Preheat the oven to 350°F. Grease a 13 x 9 x 2-inch baking pan and line the base with parchment paper.

2. Melt the chocolate and butter together in a small bowl set over a saucepan of simmering water. Let cool for 5 minutes.

3. Beat the eggs in a bowl with the vanilla extract, espresso, and sugar until well combined, then beat in the melted chocolate mix. Add the flour and salt, and beat until smooth. Crumble the hash into the mixture—it can be in chunky bits if you want. Stir in with the roughly chopped nuts. Pour the brownie mixture into the prepared baking pan.

4. Bake in the preheated oven for 25–30 minutes. Be careful not to overcook; the sides should be firm but the center still slightly soft.

5. Let cool for 10 minutes before cutting into squares. Lift the brownies out carefully with a spatula. Serve slightly warm with heavy cream, or cool completely and store in an airtight container between layers of parchment or waxed paper.

WHO ATE ALL THE HASH BROWNIES?

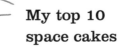

My top 10 space cakes

1
2
3
4
5
6
7
8
9
10

HIGH DESIGN

Bongs

Your bowl, your chillum, the water pipe, Ol' Faithful, Mama Goodtimes—whatever you want to call it, a well-loved bong is like a best friend. And the best bit about this best friend? If you completely destroy her by accidentally dropping her head first on the kitchen floor … you can just build a new one! It takes a bit of practical knowhow (i.e. an internet connection) to be able to do it, but in theory, the only limit is your imagination! And physics.

Bongs also make great party pieces, as you attempt to see what outlandish objects you can turn into a passage to paradise.

Did you know a homemade bong is called a mystery horn?

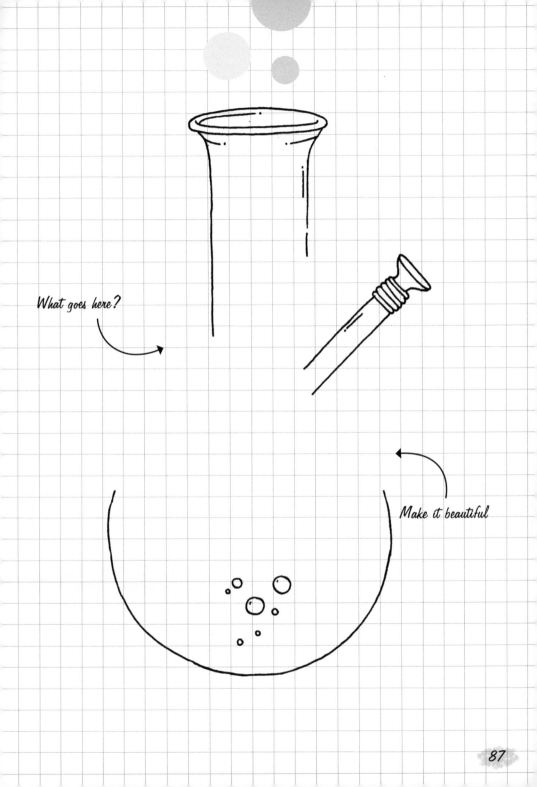

What goes here?

Make it beautiful

HOW TO ROLL A DIAMOND

For as long as anyone can remember (or at least until second-wave feminism rocked up), diamonds have been a girl's best friend. Guys? Well, they apparently get dogs to pal up with, which doesn't seem that much of a fair trade. Anyhow, now we can all settle our differences like adults, with a huge toke that is totally equal opportunities. This is a great show-stopper, and if you've got two types of weed, you can pack a sneaky change of scenery into the middle.

Keep on rollin'

1. Roll a reasonably thick joint with a decent roach. Make sure it's tightly packed.

2. Cut it in half with a sharp knife or scissors. Make sure you swing straight and true though, or you'll end up with a marijuana massacre. The ends should be clean, with no excess paper. If you've packed it tight enough, you shouldn't lose too much weed out of the cut ends either.

3. Roll two more joints, slightly looser this time, and using less weed in the center so that they've got room to bend. Trim off any excess paper, so that the weed comes right to the edge.

4. Take 10 new papers and cut off the gummed strips (use the widest you can find).

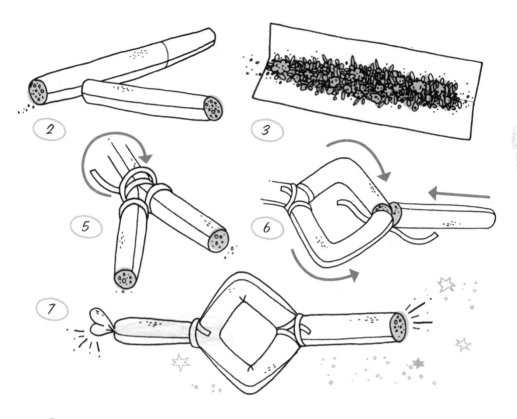

5. Ve-e-e-ry carefully, take the half of the first joint that contains the roach and attach the two looser joints to the cut end. Using a gummed strip, secure the join in a figure-eight pattern around the two joints. Repeat with another four strips, or until your joint looks solid enough to pass without disintegrating.

6. Gently bend the two looser joints at the center, until their ends meet to form a diamond shape.

7. Take the end half of the first joint and, using a gummed strip, secure the two looser joints to it in the same way as above. Spark up!

MY HIGH TIMES

What's the occasion?

_____

_____

_____

How'd you get high?

- Massive spliff
- Bong-wards
- Beautiful brownies
- Mystery box!!!

Who was there?

_____

_____

_____

(... and who brought the hash?)

_____

_____

Best highs

_____

_____

_____

Any lows?

_____

_____

_____

My favorite party costumes

Best party I've been to

I COULD TOTALLY DO THAT

Superheroes

The stoner represents nothing if not the little guy who sticks it to the Man, the dude who can blaze a trail all night and still get up the next ... afternoon. You and your friends are probably feeling pretty super right now, and you're definitely flying pretty high. So why not cook up your own superhero alter ego?

What's your superpower?

And your name?

(to strike fear into the hearts of supervillains)

Fatal flaw

(no cheating, everyone's got to have one)

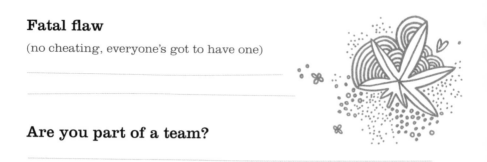

Are you part of a team?

Do you have a sidekick?

Who's your arch rival/evil nemesis?

Sketch your crime-fighting costume

(capes and hot pants are compulsory)

Tightey-Whitey:
he hurls through the air
with the greatest of ease.
Faster than a speeding
bullet (when he's running
for the bathroom), he also
has LASER VISION!
Oh no, wait, that's just
some crazy red-eye.

HIGH DESIGN

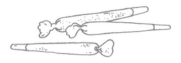

Smoke rings

However much we'd like to be that guy puffing perfect circles in the corner, we can't all be Gandalf in **Lord of the Rings**, bending the random fluctuations of air and smoke to our magical will. Our tongues are the wrong shape, our mouths are too flabby, whatever, it's just not happening.

Of course, you can practice on your own time (see page 32), but that requires a certain amount of work on your part, and maybe you haven't perfected the art yet. But here's what we would've done, right?! Right.

POT PARTY GAMES

There's every excuse for idleness when you're high—doing nothing becomes the best nothing you've ever done—but if you and your friends are at a loose end after a session, here are some very excellent (and, hallelujah, easy to follow) party games for the cannabically-inclined.

Traffic lights

Also known as Time Bomb, Mexican Sweat, or Baseball, this is a very laid-back game, but has the added bonus of making sure nobody's hogging the bong without starting a fight.

In a smoking circle (a technical term that means "sit in a regular circle," dumbass), light up a fat one (or bong), inhale, and pass it on. You have to hold your hit in until the weed makes it all the way round the circle and comes back to you. If you cough, exhale, or collapse in a fit of hysteria at somebody else's face, you lose.

Who am I?

This is a game of skill, intelligence, and memory—so should only be attempted when everybody's so wasted they keep getting up and then forgetting why.

Give each person a rolling paper and use it to write the name of a celebrity, famous character, author, royalty, TV chef, notorious drug dealer—it doesn't matter, so long as everybody there will know who that person is (don't ask, though, you'll give the game away).

Stick your named paper on another player's forehead. The players take it in turns to ask yes/no questions about who they are, like "Am I male?", "Am I rich?", "Am I a notorious drug dealer?". If you get a yes, you can have another question. A no, and you move on to the next player. The winner is, shockingly, the first person to guess their name.

Sounds pretty simple, but the golden rule is NO REMINDERS, and NO DISCUSSION. If you forget an answer, tough. If you forget who you thought it was, tough. If you go to the toilet and the paper falls off and you flush it away and nobody else can remember who you were either, TOUGH. You lose.

Weed poker

Everybody has their own joint. The first player takes a certain number of tokes and holds them in for a number of seconds (start low, like 1 toke, 3 seconds). The next person has to either up the number of tokes, or the time they hold it in for (but not both). The game goes around in a circle until somebody coughs/laughs/exhales too early/taps out.

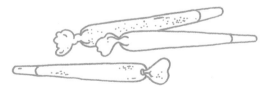

DEATHMATCH

This is a game that's uniquely suited to the kind of critical thinking and analytical skills that three hours puffing on a bong with your friends can bring you. **Alien vs. Predator** and **Freddie vs. Jason** were just the Hollywood-flavored tip of the iceberg in the age-old stoner question of "Who would win between ..." and then inserting two random names, be they poisonous snakes or obscure Japanese manga villains, video game characters or Disney princesses (or any combination of the above). Kind of like being on the debate team, but with more pot and only in terms of gruesome violence ...

Here's a few suggestions of ultimate showdowns to kick off with, so choose two and argue it out between you, but don't hold back if you come up with your own secret weapons. Once you've done a few, start fighting the winners against one another league-style, and see who comes out as the ultimate "Who would win?" victor.

Animal kindgom

Shark, piranha, T-rex, tiger, red ant colony, polar bear, rhino, black widow spider, boa constrictor, Portuguese man o' war

Supernatural creatures

Dragon, Cthulhu (look him up), vampire, werewolf, alien (assorted), troll, meddlesome gnome, genie

Historical figures

Genghis Khan, Alexander the Great, Rasputin, Queen Victoria, Abe Lincoln, Al Capone, Cleopatra

Pop legends

Lady Gaga, Slash, Marilyn Manson, The Beatles, Elvis (fat or thin), James Brown, Tina Turner, Britney Spears

Baddies

Scar from **The Lion King**, Sauron, Ming the Merciless, Darth Vader, Hannibal Lecter, Wicked Witch of the West, Norman Bates, Freddy Krueger

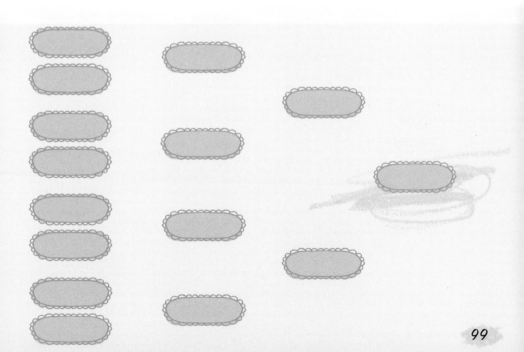

MY HIGH TIMES

What's the occasion?

_____

_____

_____

How'd you get high?

- Massive spliff
- Bong-wards
- Beautiful brownies
- Mystery box!!!

Who was there?

_____

_____

_____

(... and who brought the hash?)

_____

_____

Best highs

_____

_____

Any lows?

_____

_____

_____

Best lines of the night

(verbal, not … y'know, coke)

_____

_____

_____

_____

_____

_____

Any pranksters?

_____

_____

_____

_____

_____

_____

_____

_____

_____

_____

_____

_____

_____

_____

_____

_____

_____

* Why not?

Everybody loves a whoopee cushion!

HIGH DESIGN

Guitar

It's no secret that some of the greatest musicians of our time—
Hendrix, Marley, Dylan—have turned to the herb on occasion for a
little creative help. And it worked! The fancy fretwork of Hendrix or
Dylan's antiestablishment anthems all have an unmistakable Mary
Jane flavor—as evidenced by how excellent a soundtrack they make
to any stoner session. If you fancy yourself a bit of a guitar hero too,
design your own lean, mean, rocking machine (the guitar kind, not
the chair kind).

My dream guitar

I COULD TOTALLY DO THAT

Music festival

Now you've got your custom guitar lined up, go one better and design your own week-long music-fest! Whether it's a laid-back Woodstock-style affair, or a Burning Man week-long rave, picture yourself packing up your pot and seeing the greatest artists of our generation, all through a blissful herbal haze.

What's it called?

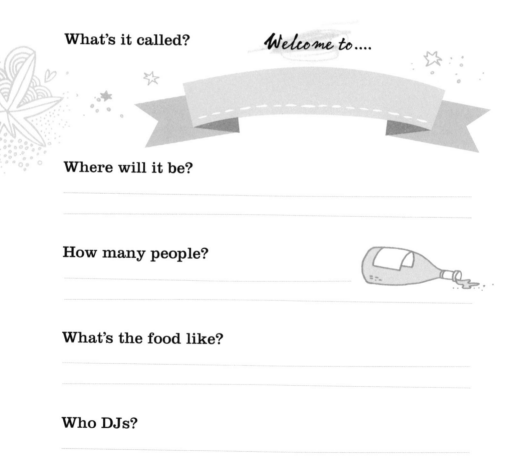

Welcome to....

Where will it be?

How many people?

What's the food like?

Who DJs?

Design your tent

Your dream line-up

What else is on offer?

> If you remember Woodstock, you weren't really there

RECIPE

Pot pizza

A savory treat for unsavory characters, this is a pizza with added pizzazz and will save you calling for takeout at one in the morning then stumbling around looking for change to pay the delivery boy. Make a couple and you've got finger food for as many hungry stoners as you can fit in your living room. Also suitable for vegetarians (after all, your body is a temple).

Pizza base:

- $1/28$ oz blond hash
- 2 cups self-rising flour
- 3 tablespoons olive oil
- 1 teaspoon salt

Topping:

- Scant $1/2$ cup full-fat cream cheese
- Scant $1/2$ cup sour cream
- 2 teaspoons freshly chopped rosemary
- 3 tablespoons olive oil
- 1 large onion, finely sliced
- $7^1/2$ cups baby spinach
- Salt and pepper

Serves **4**

1. Preheat the oven to 450°F. Grease a large baking sheet.

2. For the pizza base, put the hash and flour in a bowl with the oil and salt. Add a scant $1/2$ cup water and mix to a soft dough, adding a little more water if the dough is too dry. Roll out the dough on a lightly floured work surface into a round about 11 inches in diameter. Place on the prepared baking sheet and bake in the preheated oven for 3–4 minutes until a crust has formed.

3. For the topping, beat together the cream cheese, sour cream, rosemary, and a little salt and pepper. Heat the oil in a skillet and fry the onion for 3–4 minutes until softened. Stir in the spinach and a little salt and pepper for about 1 minute until the spinach has just wilted.

4. Pile the spinach onto the pizza base, spreading it out until about $^1/_2$ inch from the edge. Place spoonfuls of the cheese mixture on top of the spinach, then bake the pizza for 8 minutes or until turning golden.

WHO ATE ALL THE POT PIZZA?

— — — — — — — —
— — — — — — — —
— — — — — — — —
— — — — — — — —
— — — — — — — —
— — — — — — — —
— — — — — — — —
— — — — — — — —
— — — — — — — —
— — — — — — — —

My top 10 pizza toppings

1 ——————————
2 ——————————
3 ——————————
4 ——————————
5 ——————————
6 ——————————
7 ——————————
8 ——————————
9 ——————————
10 —————————

MY HIGH TIMES

What's the occasion?

How'd you get high?

- Massive spliff
- Bong-wards
- Beautiful brownies
- Mystery box!!!

Who was there?

(... and who brought the hash?)

Best highs

Any lows?

Blooper reel

(who made a total ass of themselves?)

Any dancing queens?

Who passed out before bedtime?

DOT-TO-DOT

… if you need this concept explaining to you, you're probably more stoned than you realized. Just join the dots, dumbass. Or you could design your own dot-to-dot below.

Whaddya mean they're supposed to make a picture?

2 ●

1 ●

4 ●

3 ●   5 ●

6 ●

7 ●

8 ●

10 ●

9 ●   17 ●

16 ●

14 ●

11 ●   12 ●

15 ●   18 ●

13 ●

19 ●

20 ●

21 ●   22 ●   38 ●

39 ●

23 ●   37 ●

40 ●

24 ●   27 ●   36 ●

35 ●

25 ●

26 ●

28 ●   34 ●

32 ●

33 ●

31 ●

29 ●

30 ●